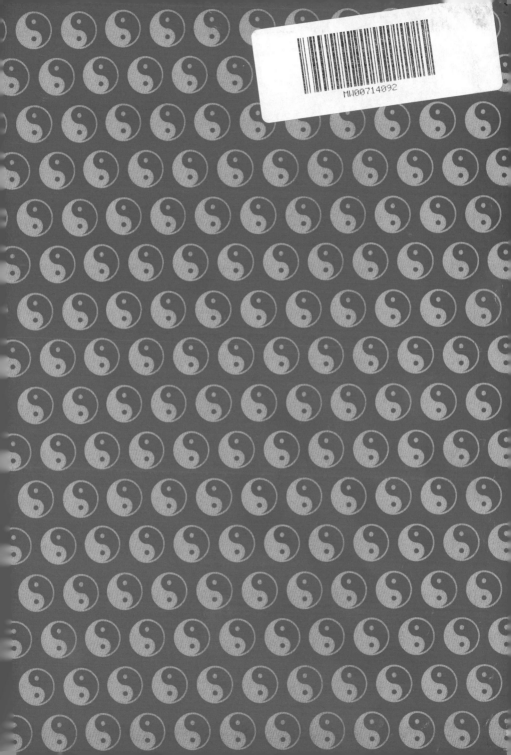

Friendship that withstands the test of time sees many things around it wither. But in each other's eyes friends only become lovelier over time.

The best gift anyone could ever give to themselves is the gift of a friend.

Our friends not only know all about us, but
they take the huge leap of loving us despite it.

Our friends in this lifetime are our guardian angels heaven sent.

A true friend can be trusted with your life and your wallet.

There is no safer feeling than the comfort of sheltering
from life's storms in the harbor of friendship.

Friendship is the shortest distance between two hearts.

_____

_____

_____

_____

_____

_____

_____

_____

_____

_____

_____

_____

_____

_____

_____

_____

_____

_____

_____

_____

_____

_____

 Life is to be fortified by many friendships. To love and to
be loved is the greatest happiness of existence.
Sydney Smith

Your friend will sing out your praises, yield to your superior
abilities, applaud your wisdom, and ignore your advice.

It is a wonderful thing to see friendship in action and experience two friends each intent on promoting the good and happiness of the other.

Nothing can sweeten the soul more effectively than friendship.

A best friend overlooks your failings and tolerates your successes.

The road to a friend's house is never long.

In the company of friends we are free to be as mad as March hares.

Make hay while the sunshine of friendship is upon you.

Two friends may be close, but just because one hurts
their foot, the other should not be expected to limp.

Chance made us friends, but with time
we may become as close as siblings.

Best friends will rarely, if ever, tell one another that they are best friends. It is simply a fact known to them both.

You may know anyone by the company they choose to keep.

Friends will always find a feast, even where there are only onions and water.

Friends pick us up when we fall, and if they cannot,
they lie down beside us and listen for a while.

_____

_____

_____

_____

_____

_____

_____

_____

_____

_____

_____

_____

_____

_____

_____

_____

_____

_____

_____

_____

_____

_____

Friendship is the warmest, most comforting bosom
in which to bury one's head in times of sorrow.

More grows in the fields of friendship than either friend will ever sow.

A friend is the icing on life's cake.

How rare and wonderful is that flash of a moment
when we realize we have discovered a friend.

William E. Rothschild

When two friends have willing hearts, nothing is impossible to them.

To live a great life, one leaves it knowing one has had good friends.

The house of friendship should be kept in a constant state of repair.

Friendship is a work of art, and should always
be displayed in the best light possible.

Our greatest glories are measured in our friends.

True friends have the strength of character to acknowledge each other's stronger and weaker points while remaining in perfect harmony.

_____

_____

_____

_____

_____

_____

_____

_____

_____

_____

_____

_____

_____

_____

_____

_____

_____

_____

_____

_____

_____

_____

_____

 What better way is there of proving that we believe in someone
than to entrust them with our friendship and our hearts?

Our friends take us as we are—
The rough with the smooth
The chaff with the grain
The sweet and the sour.

When everybody else says go, your friend will tell you to stay.

Friendship is a single tree under which many can enjoy the shade.

_____

_____

_____

_____

_____

_____

_____

_____

_____

_____

_____

_____

_____

_____

_____

_____

_____

_____

_____

_____

_____

True friendship lasts forever and everyone wants it, but few understand that to get a true friend one must become a true friend.

If you want one year of prosperity, grow grain.
If you want ten years of prosperity, grow fruit trees.
If you want a lifetime of prosperity, grow friends.

Friendship is not necessary to life, but it
does increase its value a thousand fold.

Sometimes it takes the arrival of friendship
in our lives to show us who we really are.

Friendship has us taking less than we
need and giving more than we can afford.

Good times are even better when they're shared.

Ask a friend for water and they'll try to give you an ocean.

Many a good friendship is made along the way
through life—each is a stepping stone to happiness.

Friendship is the freedom to express ourselves to another, never having to weigh our thoughts, never having to measure our words.

Plant your friendship good and deep so that it cannot be uprooted.

_____

_____

_____

_____

_____

_____

_____

_____

_____

_____

_____

_____

_____

_____

_____

_____

_____

_____

_____

_____

 With the sweet memory of a friend carried in our hearts,
we can reunite through simple meditation.

Friendship is like a recorded symphony—we may press the pause button from time to time, but release it and it's just as good as it was before.

People tend to hear what they want to hear—a true friend
always knows what it was that you meant to say.

Hold a true friend with all your might.

Life without friendship would be like waking to darkness every morning.

Friendship is pure distilled love.

A good long talk with a friend can cure almost anything.

Friends have forgiving natures, especially when it comes to our mistakes.

If you are going to bank on your friendship, then
you must occasionally make a few deposits.

Friendship is two people enjoying each
others company in the comfort of silence.

 Let us be grateful to people who make us happy; they are the charming gardeners who make our souls blossom.

Marcel Proust

_____

_____

_____

_____

_____

_____

_____

_____

_____

_____

_____

_____

_____

_____

_____

_____

_____

_____

_____

_____

_____

My best friend is not only my best friend—my best friend is my second self.

Friends are always close to each other's hearts,
even if they are on opposite sides of the globe.

Let the crystal waters of friendship wash over you
and cleanse away all the baneful vexations of life.

Somewhere out there is someone who was born to be your friend.

One of the most reassuring feelings is knowing our friends
will always be there to help us, should we need them.

Friendship is that voice in your heart that tells you all is well, that you are being guarded and guided, and that you should feel no fear.

Friendship is built upon constructive thoughts and positive actions.

_____

_____

_____

_____

_____

_____

_____

_____

_____

_____

_____

_____

_____

_____

_____

_____

_____

_____

_____

_____

_____

_____

_____

_____

 Our friends will always find the vein of gold
that runs, un-mined, deep within us.

Do everything that you do in this life in the spirit of friendship.
For friendship is the seed, and the universe is the tree.

Old friends are like old shoes—infinitely more comfortable.

Friendship is a tough nut to crack, but the flesh is sweet.

It is a good thing to be rich, and a good thing to be strong,
but it is a better thing to be beloved of many friends.

Euripides

We can only be wise alone if we occasionally
balance it by going a bit wild with a friend.

The time you enjoy wasting with your friends is not wasted time.

The most accessible pleasure is talking with good friends.
It is the best value communication that exists.

Life is a great stealer of time, and friendship requires as
much as we can give it. Respect your friends and celebrate
friendships with time spent in their good company.

Friends are our partners in the dance of life,
not to be dropped when the ball ends.

One should never close one's heart and
mind off to the possibility of friendship.

A friendship is built out of caring, sharing, and giving.
It is something very special that just happens to us one
fine day and remains with us for the rest of our lives.

We love our friends not only for being themselves,
but also for what we are when we are with them.

You ask me what I am worth? It can only be measured in friendships.

Going through life with a friend is a true education.

Walking along through life in friendship is a journey steeped in wonder.

Pure friendship is boundless and infinite. Once we have
gained this understanding there is nothing more to try
to understand; it is better simply to relax and enjoy it.

Start the day with thoughts of a friend.

Friendship is based upon pure thoughts and a
pure heart, true devotion and outstretched arms.

A friend wipes away our tears of grief and replaces them with tears of joy.

Friendship is the free expression of people's unshakeable love for each other—love that is pure, noble, and free from desire for personal gain.

Life without friendship is like swimming without water.

Friendship is the swiftest path to contentment—
and there is no greater provider of happiness than that.

Friendship must emanate from the heart, for that is
where it resides—next to peace, trust, and faith.

Like good wine, where the friendship is the oldest there is the greatest trust.

Nothing is more entire and without reserve, more zealous, contented, affectionate, or sincere than the constancy of friendship.

Seen through the eyes of our friendship, all things
and all beings can become beautiful.

When troubles come, look beyond the dark
clouds to the blue skies of friendship.

We go through life alone thinking we are the only one who feels a certain way about things, and then suddenly someone comes along who feels exactly the same way. It's the start of a beautiful friendship.

When a close friendship is formed with another
it is as if there were one mind in two bodies.

Friendship waits outside like the sun's rays. It takes us
to open the door for its light to flood into your life.

12 The Ivories · 6–8 Northampton Street · London N1 2HY
Tel: +44 (0)20 7359 2244 · Fax: +44 (0)20 7359 1616 · mail@mqpublications.com
www.mqpublications.com

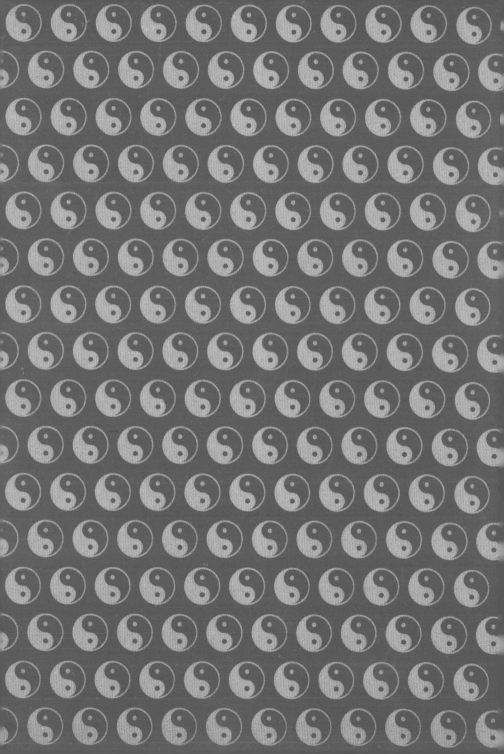